UNCOVERING
AMERICAN HISTORY™

A PRIMARY SOURCE INVESTIGATION OF
THE ERIE CANAL

LARA SAHGAL
AND JANEY LEVY

rosen publishing's
rosen
central®

Published in 2016 by The Rosen Publishing Group, Inc.
29 East 21st Street, New York, NY 10010

Copyright © 2016 by The Rosen Publishing Group, Inc.

First Edition

Library of Congress Cataloging-in-Publication Data

Sahgal, Lara.
A primary source investigation of the Erie Canal/Lara Sahgal and Janey Levy.—First edition.
    pages cm.—(Uncovering American history)
Includes bibliographical references and index.
ISBN 978-1-4994-3509-2 (library bound)
1. Erie Canal (N.Y.)—History—Juvenile literature. I. Levy, Janey. II. Title.
HE396.E6S24 2016
386'.4809747—dc23

                                                    2014046416

Manufactured in the United States of America

CONTENTS

INTRODUCTION

Despite the number of hours many of us spend commuting using highly advanced infrastructure, few of us can imagine writing songs about a highway or subway line. Yet after the Erie Canal was completed in 1825, it became the subject of numerous songs, stories, books, poems, and more. It was not the first canal built in the United States. So what was it about the man-made waterway that captured the imagination of so many?

Part of the answer lies in the scope of the construction project itself. With the Louisiana Purchase in 1803, the size of the United States nearly doubled, which meant that settlers began moving to the new territories and merchants became eager to sell—and transport—their goods to them. However, travel to these areas required crossing the Appalachian Mountains, which presented great difficulties. In 1807, a flour merchant named Jesse Hawley proposed a canal 363 miles (584 kilometers)

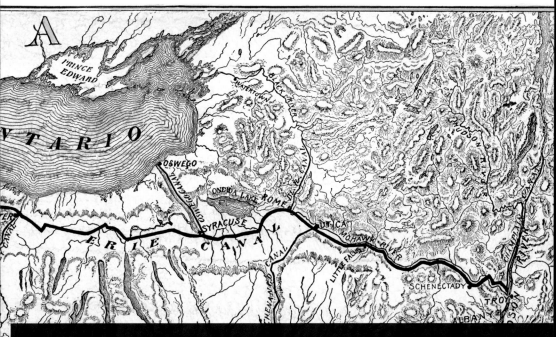

This hand-colored woodcut map from the 1800s shows the areas through which the original Erie Canal passed. Although it has been modified over time, it can still be seen in many of these locations.

long—more than twelve times the length of the longest U.S. canal at the time—that would connect the Hudson River, in the eastern part of New York State, to Lake Erie, in the western part, allowing easier travel across the Appalachians.

New York governor DeWitt Clinton was an early supporter of the project. In 1817, he convinced the state to spend $7 million on the Erie Canal project. He faced a great deal of criticism, with many calling the canal "Clinton's Folly" or "Clinton's Ditch," but when the project was completed in 1825, it was an almost instant success, inspiring in people a feeling of possibility, prosperity, and nationalism.

As a result of the project, innovative new technologies were introduced, and the economies of cities and towns across New York—New York City not the least among them—were boosted dramatically. Bringing together individuals from all walks of life, the Erie Canal also represented more than the exchange of goods and products—it was also a means of cultural exchange. While the economic impact of the Erie Canal has declined, it remains an iconic part of the geographic and cultural landscape of the United States, continuing to inspire visitors and admirers to this day.

CHAPTER ONE

FROM DREAM TO DITCH

Several proposals to build canals to improve the transportation of goods across New York State had been suggested since the 1780s. The first canal project in New York, which was designed to connect the Hudson River to Lake Ontario, was started on the Mohawk River in 1792. The end result, however, was a one-mile-long (1.6 km) canal that allowed ships to navigate Little Falls. The larger issue—that of transporting goods and settlers across longer distances—remained. It would take the determination and vision of one flour merchant to help make the much grander Erie Canal project a reality.

INSPIRATION FROM DESPERATION

Jesse Hawley was a flour merchant in Geneva, New York. He had to pay such high prices to transport his flour by wagon that he couldn't make any money. He struggled so much, in fact, that he went bankrupt and was sent to debtors' prison.

In 1807, after several months of studying maps of New York State, Hawley figured out a route for a canal connecting Lake Erie in western New York with the Hudson River in the eastern part of the state. This would provide a cheap, fast way to ship goods to settlers around the Great Lakes and in the territories gained as part of the Louisiana Purchase. Supplies such as crockery, sugar, molasses, coffee, nails, spikes, iron, and steel would travel up the Hudson River from New York City, across the state on the canal, then across the Great Lakes to settlers. Agricultural products from the settlers would follow the route in the opposite direction to reach the eastern markets.

Hawley published essays about his idea in the *Genesee Messenger* in 1807 and 1808. A New York State senator named DeWitt Clinton read Hawley's essays in the newspaper and decided that Hawley was right.

AN ESSAY

ON THE

ENLARGEMENT

OF THE

ERIE CANAL,

WITH ARGUMENTS IN FAVOR OF RETAINING THE PRESENT
PROPOSED SIZE OF SEVENTY FEET BY SEVEN; AND
FOR ITS ENTIRE LENGTH FROM ALBANY TO
BUFFALO WITHOUT ANY DIMINUTION.

BY JESSE HAWLEY.

Jesse Hawley's sustained interest in the project he helped initiate is evident in this 1840 essay, which makes recommendations for ways to enlarge and improve the canal. (For a transcription, see page 49.)

JESSE HAWLEY

A businessman with no engineering or surveying background who was struggling to maintain his flour business, Jesse Hawley proved to be an unexpected source for one of the most momentous ideas in American history. Born in 1742, Hawley worked as a flour merchant in Canandaigua, New York. He later moved to Lockport. Hawley's business required him to transport flour east over dirt roads that were variously muddy or dusty and often full of ruts and potholes. To make matters worse, high tolls and the decay of goods during the long, arduous trip were bad for business.

Hawley began to envision alternate routes and hit upon the idea of a canal. He discussed the idea with one of his suppliers and then James Geddes, a surveyor who would go on to work on the Erie Canal when the project was underway. Hawley realized that Lake Erie could serve as the head of water that would feed the canal. He reasoned that using Lake Ontario might involve including British and Canadian officials. Using Lake Erie, there could be a direct route with no outside influence. Hawley did research on canals in Europe and calculated the type of traffic the Erie project might draw as well as the costs and economic benefits. He even projected the types of supplies needed and methods that could be used

(continued on the next page)

(continued from the previous page)

in construction and mapped a detailed route of a possible canal, much of which was used when the project was finally adopted.

In the meantime, however, Hawley and his partner began to build up debt and eventually went bankrupt. They fled to Pittsburgh, Pennsylvania, to escape their creditors. Hawley decided to return to New York and was then sent to debtors' prison for twenty months in Canandaigua. While in Pittsburgh, he had written a newspaper article about the canal project. In prison, Hawley expanded these ideas into a series of essays published in the local newspaper, the *Genessee Messenger*, under the pen name, Hercules. The essays ran from 1807 to 1808.

Eloquent and convincing, Hawley's message soon found an audience with DeWitt Clinton, who would go on to be elected governor of New York. Clinton would make Hawley's dream a reality and an instant success.

Hawley spoke at the opening celebration for the Erie Canal on October 26, 1825. From 1836 to 1842, he was the treasurer of Lockport. Hawley died in 1842 and is buried not far from the Erie Canal, at Cold Spring Cemetery.

GAINING TRACTION

Although many dismissed Hawley's essays, a few key figures took note. In 1808, a New York State assemblyman, Joshua Forman, proposed legislation that called for surveyors to examine the route between Lake Erie and the

Hudson River to gauge if a canal would even be possible and desirable. In 1810, state senator Jonas Platt partnered with the treasurer of the Western Inland Lock Navigation Company, Thomas Eddy, to discuss the idea with DeWitt Clinton, then a highly respected and influential state senator.

Clinton quickly became actively involved in advocating for the canal. In 1810, Clinton became the canal commissioner of New York. To raise public support for a canal throughout the state, Clinton gave speeches and wrote a letter to the state legislature. His influence helped pass a measure in the state senate that

This portrait of DeWitt Clinton was painted by John Wesley Jarvis c. 1820, a few years after he assumed the office of governor.

called for commissioners to survey the canal route. In spite of his efforts, many people thought the idea was foolish, calling it "Clinton's Folly" or "Clinton's Ditch." Nonetheless, Clinton remained convinced that it would work. When he was elected governor of New York in 1817, he persuaded the state legislature to authorize $7 million to build the canal. Work on the canal began later that year.

DEWITT CLINTON

DeWitt Clinton served in numerous political positions, at the local, state, and national levels, accomplishing much in his illustrious career, but he remains best known as the "father of the Erie Canal." Clinton was born on March 2, 1769, in Little Britain, New York. His uncle was George Clinton, who served as governor of New York for twenty-one years and as vice president under two different presidents.

After graduating from Columbia College in 1786, Clinton practiced law. In 1790, he began serving as his uncle's private secretary, launching his long career in government. He was elected to the New York State Assembly in 1797. He then went on to serve in several other positions. At the state level, he was state senator (1792–1802), lieutenant governor (1811–13), and governor (1817–23; 1825–28). At the local level, he was mayor of New York City (1803–15 except for two annual terms). He also served nationally as a U.S. senator (1802–03).

Clinton worked intensively on the Erie Canal project after learning of Hawley's letters and meeting with Platt and Eddy. He sought federal aid, but after facing refusal in Washington, he turned to the state for support. In 1816 the state legislature decided to fund the canal. In 1817, Clinton was elected governor of New York, which allowed him to manage and stay involved with the project.

After the successful completion of the Erie Canal project in 1825 and its subsequent flourishing, Clinton was credited with helping transform New York City and other towns in the state into vibrant centers of culture and trade.

In addition to his interest in the canal, Clinton is remembered for his varying and widespread accomplishments. As mayor, he supported free public education and institutions for public welfare. He also maintained an avid interest in arts, culture, and science, even publishing a work about science. Clinton died on February 11, 1828, in Albany.

A RESOUNDING SUCCESS

"Clinton's Ditch" was finished in 1825, and a great celebration to mark the canal's completion began on October 26 and continued for nine days. In Buffalo, Governor Clinton led a parade of nearly all of the city's five thousand residents down to the western end of the "grand canal." After giving speeches, Governor Clinton, Lieutenant Governor James Tallmadge Jr., and other distinguished citizens of the state boarded a canal boat named the *Seneca Chief* and set off for New York City. On the journey, Clinton carried a keg of water from Lake Erie; he would pour it into the Atlantic Ocean in a ceremony when they reached New York Harbor. Cannons had been placed every 10 miles (16 km) along the canal. When the *Seneca Chief* began its journey, the first cannon was fired.

In Charles Yardley Turner's *Marriage of the Waters*, DeWitt Clinton pours a keg of water from Lake Erie into the Atlantic Ocean, symbolically joining the two bodies of water, as the Erie Canal had done.

Once the men at the second cannon heard the noise of the first cannon, they fired their cannon. Eighty minutes later, the last cannon fired in New York City.

Towns across the state celebrated the Erie Canal. On November 4, 1825, nine days after leaving Buffalo, the *Seneca Chief* reached New York Harbor. A magnificent ceremony marked the boat's arrival. More than one hundred thousand people crowded the shores. Clinton made a speech and then poured the keg of Lake Erie water into the Atlantic Ocean. This "marriage of the waters" symbolized the joining of Lake Erie and the Atlantic Ocean by the Erie Canal.

CHAPTER TWO

THE ERIE SCHOOL OF ENGINEERS

The Erie Canal is remembered in large part for the innovative solutions its engineers found to the numerous challenges the construction presented. This is especially impressive considering that the project was completed at a time when the United States had no engineering schools. Few of the individuals involved in the construction had any experience with engineering, and all had to learn the ins and outs of canal building as they went along. Yet throughout the course of the project, new machines and devices were invented to aid construction, and in the end, the surveyors and engineers who came together to make the canal a reality were hailed as the "Erie School of Engineers." Together, they ushered in a new age of technological achievement, which saw the rise of new vital infrastructure—including networks of canals and railroads—throughout the United States.

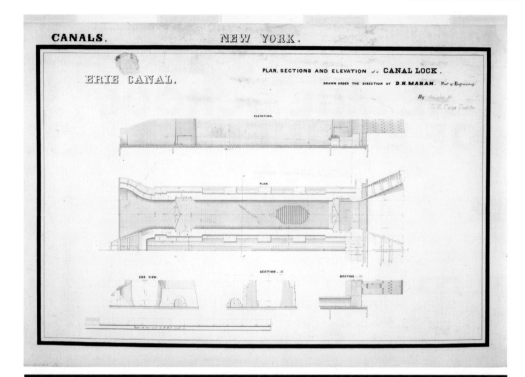

CANALS.   NEW YORK.

ERIE CANAL.

PLAN, SECTIONS AND ELEVATION OF CANAL LOCK.

DRAWN UNDER THE DIRECTION OF **D. H. MAHAN.** Prof. of Engineering

The Erie Canal was an important area of study in many engineering programs established after its completion. This c. 1855 drawing of a lock on the canal was done by West Point cadet Orlando Metcalfe Poe.

PAVING THE WAY

Before construction on the canal could begin, land had to be cleared. To facilitate this, the engineers designed a machine that made it possible for one man working alone to bring down a tree quickly, without using a saw or an axe. This was achieved in the following way: one end of a cable was attached to the top of a tree while the other end was attached to an endless screw. The cable was wound around the screw by turning a wheel. Turning the wheel pulled the top of the tree lower and lower, until finally the tree came down.

To pull out the stumps left behind, a stump puller was invented. This device consisted of a winch (a machine that can pull or lift heavy things with a chain) with 18-foot (5.5-meter) wheels. Once the chain was tied around the stump, the winch could be turned. With this, a crew of six men and some horses could then clear an average of forty trees each day.

Other clearing tools that emerged as a result of the Erie Canal were a greatly improved wheelbarrow and a new plow that helped clear roots under the soil. As the canal project wore on, even greater technological marvels would emerge.

A CRACK TEAM

The canal was divided into three main sections: eastern, middle, and western. Each portion presented a unique set of challenges, natural and otherwise. Construction on the middle portion began on July 4, 1817, in Rome, New York.

At the helm of the canal's construction were four individuals appointed by the canal commissioners. After abandoning their search for foreign experts with experience in canal construction in Europe, the commissioners took a different approach. They turned to four surveyors in New York. None were actually surveyors by trade—three were judges and one was a schoolteacher—and none had seen, let alone built, a canal before.

But the decision was not as far-fetched as it may seem. No formal engineering programs were in existence at the time. Additionally, it was common for judges and lawyers to study surveying in order to settle disputes involving deeds, leases, and other property-related issues. The four men— Benjamin Wright, James Geddes, Nathan Roberts, and Charles Brodhead—alongside teams of other talented individuals, would soon prove themselves worthy of the task.

SURVEYING

Surveying is the practice of determining measurements of the earth's surfaces. The art of surveying has been in existence in various forms since ancient times, with tools and techniques evolving over the centuries. It remains a critical consideration in such areas as building construction and transportation. Surveyors must be able to make precise measurements.

In the early nineteenth century, many lawyers and judges would study simple surveying, which involved determining measurements in relatively small areas. Surveying for canal construction was significantly different. Surveyors would need to make very precise vertical and horizontal measurements over long distances; errors that were more than a few inches off could dramatically affect construction. Despite their inexperience, the four principal engineers of the Erie Canal project learned quickly. Benjamin Wright and James Geddes were asked to run levels on the canal course in the spring of 1818. Each took a different route from Rome to Syracuse—covering a 100-mile (160-km) loop—and then compared readings. The difference was less than 2 inches (5 centimeters).

BENJAMIN WRIGHT

Benjamin Wright, the chief engineer on the Erie Canal, was born in Wethersfield, Connecticut, in 1770. He didn't have much formal education. However, he studied law with an uncle and eventually became a judge. There were no law schools in the country at that time, and most lawyers learned law through private study. Wright's uncle also taught him how to survey, or measure, land. Land had to be surveyed before it could be bought or sold. Wright was known as an accurate and honest surveyor, and it was because of his skills and reputation that he was chosen to be chief engineer.

After completing the Erie Canal, Wright went on to design and build many other canals, including the Chesapeake and Ohio Canal and the Delaware and Hudson Canal. He was also one of the first men to design and build railroads, and he served as chief engineer of the Erie Railroad. Wright, who died in 1842, is remembered today as the father of American civil engineering.

JAMES GEDDES

James Geddes, the assistant chief engineer on the project, was born near Carlisle, Pennsylvania, in 1763. His father was a wealthy farmer, and the younger Geddes received the best education possible at the time. After several years of traveling around the eastern United States, teaching and running a business that manufactured salt, Geddes went to work as a surveyor. Like Wright, he had a reputation for accuracy, and because of this he was chosen to be the assistant chief engineer for the Erie Canal. Geddes had also been involved in promoting the idea of the canal before the state legislature officially sanctioned the project. The canal route that was eventually settled upon was close to one that he had proposed in 1808, after some surveying work he performed to help encourage the project.

Also like Wright, Geddes later worked on other canals. He was chief engineer for the Ohio Canal and the Champlain Canal, and he also worked on the Pennsylvania canals. He died in 1838. A biography of Geddes was included in Joshua V. H. Clark's book *Onondaga; or Reminiscences of Earlier and Later Times, Vol. 2*, published in Syracuse, New York, in 1849 by Stoddard and Babcock. Clark praised Geddes with these words: "His name will ever be associated with the noblest works of the age."

NATHAN ROBERTS

Nathan S. Roberts was born in Piles Grove, New Jersey, in 1776. In 1817, he was made an assistant engineer on the Erie Canal. Soon thereafter, he was put in charge of the Rome to Rochester section of the canal. Drawn by the beauty of the area, Roberts purchased a farm conveniently located near the canal in Lenox, New York, about 15 miles (24 km) east of Syracuse. He remained there until his death in 1852.

In 1822, Roberts was given the task of finding a solution to one of the greatest obstacles faced by the Erie Canal engineers. Near Niagara Falls, in the western part of New York State, a sharply rising rock cliff soared more than 70 feet (21 m) above the surrounding land. To reach Lake Erie, the engineers had to find a way to get boats up and over this high ridge.

Normally, engineers use a lock to enable boats to move between sections of a canal with different water levels.

Roberts knew that it wouldn't be possible to reach the top of the steep cliff with a single pair of locks. Accordingly, he designed a series of five double locks that resembled a giant flight of stairs. Nothing this difficult had ever been done before, and Roberts's "flight of five" became one of the canal's great wonders. Remnants of the eastbound side survive, but they are not in use; the westbound side was replaced in 1918 with a flight of two locks that handle traffic in both directions.

When construction of the locks began in 1823, 1,200 laborers, mostly Irish immigrants who were already in New York, came to work on the project. To provide the goods and services the workers needed, merchants, farmers, doctors,

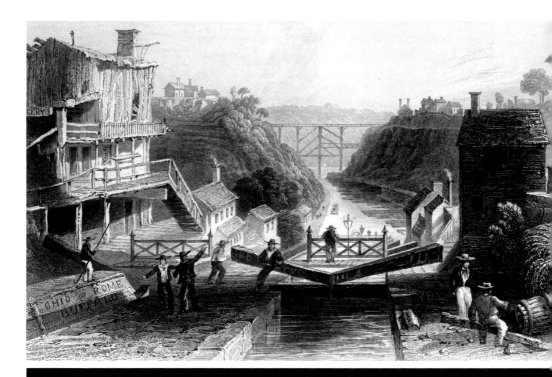

This engraving, entitled *Lockport, Erie Canal*, is based on a drawing by landscape artist William H. Bartlett, which shows workers on the Erie Canal in the town of Lockport, New York.

LOCK

A lock has a set of gates at each end. A boat going from a lower level to a higher level enters the lock through the lower gates, which are then closed behind it. Water is let into the lock to raise the boat to the level of the higher section. Then the gates at that end of the lock are opened, and the boat passes through. The process is reversed for boats moving from the higher level to the lower level. Double locks are like a two-way street, with one "lane" for boat traffic moving in one direction and another for boats moving in the opposite direction. It took only one person to operate each lock. The Erie Canal would end up requiring eighty-three locks.

and bankers soon arrived. By the time the Erie Canal opened in 1825, a town of 2,500 people had grown up around the locks. The town took its name from its famous locks and was called Lockport.

CHARLES BRODHEAD

Charles Brodhead was born on April 20, 1772, in Ulster County, New York. His surveying education began early. In the 1790s, he undertook various surveying assignments in Utica, where he had settled, and went on to complete some remarkable surveying work in often difficult terrain around the state, including the Adirondacks.

In 1816, he became the chief engineer of the eastern portion—some say the most difficult—of the Erie Canal project. Although he did not stay with the project until the end, he did ensure the completion of his portion, adding a number of locks and navigating the various issues in engineering and design that arose during the course of his work.

Brodhead died in 1852 in Utica, largely forgotten.

AS A DUCT TAKES TO WATER

One of the major problems confronting the engineers was how to get across rivers and creeks, including the Genesee River, Irondequoit Creek, and Ninemile Creek. The solution was an aqueduct bridge. An aqueduct bridge had to be wide enough for the canal itself and for the towpath along the side of it. Canal boats didn't have engines or sails. Instead, they were towed by teams of horses or mules that walked beside the canal.

The Erie Canal required eighteen aqueduct bridges. One of the longest crossed the Genesee River at Rochester. More than 800 feet (245 m) long, it was built of huge stones, all of which had to

This rendering shows the Erie Canal's aqueduct bridge at Rochester, New York, in the early 1900s. The bridge was originally more than 800 feet (245 m) long and 17 feet (5 m) wide, and had 11 arches.

be quarried and shaped by hand. Like the "flight of five," the bridge at Rochester was admired as one of the most amazing accomplishments of the canal.

Another remarkable engineering innovation to come out of the project included cement that could harden underwater.

A MODERN MARVEL

The Erie Canal was completed on October 26, 1825, two years before it was actually projected to be finished. It was 363 miles (584 km) long—more than two times the length of any canal in Europe at the time. Its dimensions—40 feet (12 m) wide at the top, 28 feet (8.5 m) at the bottom, and 4 feet (1.2 m) deep—were in fact common to other canals as well. But boasting revolutionary feats of engineering and construction, the Erie Canal represented something much more: a new age of growth and progress in which people did not have to remain tethered to the limits of nature.

The canal began drawing visitors in droves and became the subject of both visual and literary works. During the second and third quarters of the nineteenth century, the Erie Canal was such a popular subject that canal scenes decorated plates, cups, bowls, wallpaper, and clothing. One man who worked on the canal even had a picture of an aqueduct carved on his gravestone. To many who saw it, the Erie Canal was the Eighth Wonder of the World.

CHAPTER THREE

A NEW AGE IS LAUNCHED

Within just nine years, the Erie Canal had paid for itself. Its immense success was fueled by the fact that boats transporting goods across the canal could carry vastly more cargo than horse-drawn wagons. This additionally lowered the cost of transport. Before the construction of the canal, it would cost $100 per ton to transport products from Buffalo to New York City. After, the cost was lowered to less than $10 per ton. The state earned income by collecting freight tolls for the goods transported on the canal. After the costs of construction

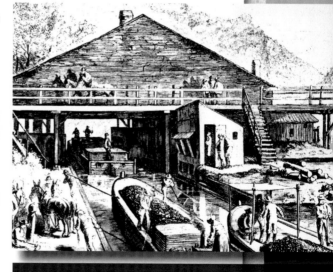

Barges arrive in New York City from Buffalo shortly after the opening of the Erie Canal, which allowed goods to be transported between the two cities much more easily and cheaply than ever before.

25

were covered, the state used these funds to build numerous other canals. Other states would soon follow suit.

CANAL FEVER

The Erie Canal was a huge success even before it was completed. In 1824, traffic on the sections that were open allowed the state of New York to collect $300,000 in tolls. In 1826, the first full year the entire canal was open for business, the state collected more than $1 million in tolls— an exceptional amount of money, especially in the 1800s. More than 185,000 tons of agricultural products, such as wheat, flour, bacon, butter, cheese, corn, and potatoes, were transported from Buffalo to Albany in 1826, and more than 32,000 tons of manufactured goods, such as furniture, nails, iron, steel, and crockery, traveled from Albany to Buffalo. By 1845, more than one million tons of freight went up and down the canal annually.

The section of the Erie Canal between Rome and Utica opened in October 1819. Its immediate success helped fuel a canal-building fever. The Champlain Canal, connecting the Hudson River and the St. Lawrence River, also opened in 1819; in 1826, a canal connecting Cayuga and Seneca lakes with the Erie Canal was completed; two years later came the Oswego Canal, linking Lake Ontario and the Erie Canal system; in 1828, the Delaware and Hudson Canal opened, joining the coal fields of Pennsylvania to the Hudson River; and in 1831, the Morris Canal in New Jersey opened, joining the Delaware River to the Hudson River. The communities along these canals grew and prospered.

BIGGER AND BETTER

By 1846, the number of boats using the canal had grown from about 170 in 1826 to about 4,000 in 1846. The

RATE CHARTS

To find out how much to charge for different kinds of freight, toll collectors used rate charts. The rates were based on three factors: distance, weight of the freight, and type of freight. The highest tolls were charged for luxury items, such as silverware, china, and fabrics like silk and velvet. The lowest tolls were for items such as brick, sand, clay, and manure. To enable the toll collector to find information quickly and easily, the charts were given a simple design.

The chart seen to the right is divided into two sides, each with information arranged in clearly labeled columns. The left side of the chart lists rates for agricultural products shipped from

(continued on the next page)

TABLE OF THE NEW RATES OF TOLL
ON THE ERIE CANAL,
As established by the Canal board, and in effect on said Canal.

Per this table, shipping a barrel of flour from Buffalo to Brockport in 1846 cost six cents, four mills, and 8.0.0 farthings. (For a transcription, see page 50.)

(*continued from the previous page*)

Buffalo to Albany. It also lists the distance from Buffalo to each port along the canal. The right side indicates rates for manufactured goods shipped from Albany to Buffalo and the distance from Albany to each port. Rates are calculated in monetary units called mills; a mill is equal to one-tenth of a cent. To figure out what the toll would be for a particular type of freight, you first had to look at the table of distances to find out how many miles the freight would be traveling. Then you would look at the toll rates to find out what the toll would be for that type of freight traveling that many miles.

Reading from left to right on the left side of the chart, the columns list distance, place name, toll for a barrel of flour, toll for 100 pounds of all items with a toll rate of four mills, all items with a rate of three mills, all items with a rate of two mills, and all items with a rate of one mill. The right side of the chart lists a column for distance, one for place name, and then one each for tolls for 100 pounds of all items with a toll rate of eight mills, all items with a rate of five mills, and all items with a rate of three mills. At the bottom of the chart is a key that lists the items covered by each toll rate.

The toll collector would post the table in a spot in his office where it would be easiest for him to consult it and quickly find the information he needed. Because the tables were in constant use, they were easily damaged and had to be replaced. New tables were printed when rates changed, and the outdated tables were thrown away. Very few toll tables exist today since they were thrown away when they were no longer needed.

number of men employed on the boats and on the canal itself had reached about 25,000. Additionally, towns along the canal flourished. The population of Utica increased from about 3,000 to about 13,000 in only twenty years. Syracuse, which consisted of only a few wooden houses in 1820, had 11,000 residents in 1840. Buffalo, a tiny wilderness settlement of about 200 in 1812, had a population of 18,000 by 1840.

Recognizing the canal's importance to the state's economy, the New York legislature decided to enlarge the canal so that it could handle bigger boats carrying more freight. Work on this project started in 1835 but came

This rendering of freight traffic on the Erie Canal along the Buffalo waterfront shows smokestacks and other signs that Buffalo by the 1880s had already transformed from a rural settlement into a bustling industrial center.

to a halt during the Depression of 1837. Banks had been loaning money to anyone who wanted it. When many people could not pay back the loans, the banks lost money. Then governments ran out of money to pay for projects like canals.

Some people in the state government thought that the state should abandon the enlargement of the canal as too expensive. Others thought the expansion was so important to the state that it should borrow money to pay for it.

Work on the enlargement resumed in 1853. By 1860, commerce on the canal had increased greatly. Altogether, almost two million tons of agricultural products were carried east from Buffalo in 1860. In 1825, only 185,000 tons of freight traveled east on the canal.

The increasing volume of freight yielded a huge financial benefit for New York State. In 1862, the year the enlargement of the Erie Canal was completed, the state collected more than $4,500,000 in tolls. Government officials and wealthy citizens in other states wanted to build canals that would help their states collect a lot of money, too.

WESTWARD HO

While the Erie Canal's clearest beneficiary was the state of New York, the canal was instrumental in shaping the development and economies of much of the nation as well. Because transport to western territories had become easier, settlers were migrating west in greater numbers. The Erie Canal was an important conduit for both settlers and goods. This meant that the canal linked northeastern states to the Midwest economically and socially—and as would be seen during the Civil War, politically as well. Midwestern states largely demonstrated support for the

Union. If trade in the Midwest remained on the Mississippi River, however, as it had before the building on the Erie Canal, New Orleans would have been an important hub, possibly creating very different loyalties during the war.

The Erie Canal also became an important part of the Underground Railroad, allowing slaves to escape from the south passage to Canada. Many towns along the canal became the sites of various cultural and reform movements. Seneca Falls, for example, was the town in which the first women's rights convention was held.

CHAPTER FOUR

THE RAILROAD AGE

The invention of the steam engine radically transformed land transport. The first railroads began in Europe, but the United States quickly followed suit. The first to be chartered in the United States was the Baltimore and Ohio Railroad, which was completed in 1852. At first, railroads seemed to serve as a complement to canal systems. The Erie Canal continued to prosper for several more years after its enlargement project was completed. By 1868, the volume of freight carried by the canal exceeded three million tons.

Increasingly, however, railroads—offering faster travel and lower maintenance costs— were challenging the canals' control over the transportation of goods. New York legislators hoped to stifle competition to the canal from the railroads by prohibiting them from carrying freight. But eventually, railroads proved to be more operational in the winter and the freight rule did not last. The hold of the Erie Canal would only continue to decline.

Baltimore & Ohio 0-4-0 Switcher

The B&O has four 0-4-0 locomotives, two of them (the 97 and the 98) tankers, and the other two (96 and 99) tender engines like the plans.

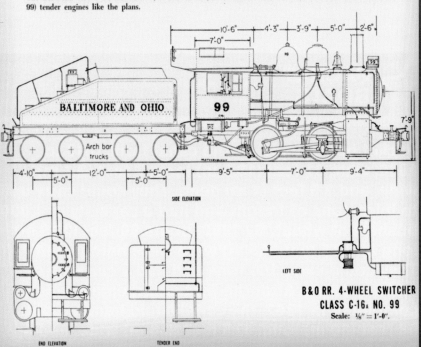

BALTIMORE AND OHIO

99

Arch bar trucks

SIDE ELEVATION

END ELEVATION

TENDER END

LEFT SIDE

B&O RR. 4-WHEEL SWITCHER CLASS C-16ₐ NO. 99
Scale: ⅛″ = 1′-0″.

The photographs and diagrams here are of railcars used by the Baltimore and Ohio Railroad in the early 1900s. The efficient design and function would quickly edge out the use of canals.

A SHORT PARTNERSHIP

In the early years of the canal age, canals and trains often formed partnerships, creating routes covered partly by train and partly by canal boat. Though these partnerships also pertained to goods, they were especially beneficial to travelers. Packet boats allowed passengers to experience the wonders of the canals and enjoy the scenery. Trains, on the other hand, were faster—packet boats moved at a speed of only 4 miles (6.5 km) per hour—and often more comfortable. However, there were very few railroads, and those that existed covered only short distances.

New York's first railroad opened in 1831, stretching 16 miles (25.7 km) from Albany to Schenectady. Passengers

PACKET BOATS

Packet boats, used on the canal from 1817 to 1830, were 61 feet (18.5 m) long, 7 feet (2.1 m) wide, and 3.5 feet (1 m) deep. They could carry up to thirty tons of freight and had a capacity of 1,000 bushels of wheat. By 1850, boats 90 feet (27.5 m) long and 15 feet (4.5 m) wide were being used. They could carry 100 tons and had a capacity of 3,333 bushels. After the first enlargement was completed in 1862, the canal could handle boats 98 feet (30 m) long, 17.5 feet (5.3 m) wide, and 6 feet (1.8 m) deep. These boats could carry 240 tons and had a capacity of 8,000 bushels of wheat!

The "suggested improvement" would create still larger boats: 125 feet (38 m) long, 17.5 feet (5.3 m) wide, and 8 feet (2.4 m) deep. These boats would be able to carry 450 tons and would have a capacity of 16,000 bushels. The "recommended enlargement" would result in even more impressive boats. They would be 150 feet (45.7 m) long, 25 feet (7.6 m) wide, and 10 feet (3 m) deep. They would be able to carry 1,000 tons and would have a capacity of 33,333 bushels of wheat.

Horse-drawn packet boats, like this one, could carry up to sixty passengers, who could ride on the roof to enjoy the view or in the cabin, which usually had sleeping and dining areas.

could take a train departing Albany at 9:00 AM or one departing at 5:00 PM. The morning train would get them to Schenectady in time to catch the packet boat leaving for Utica, Rochester, and Buffalo at 10:30 AM. The afternoon train would allow passengers to catch the packet boat leaving Schenectady at 6:30 PM. By taking the train instead of the canal from Albany to Schenectady, travelers shortened their journey by one day.

In 1836, the Utica and Schenectady Railroad was completed, making it possible to travel (or transport goods) all the way from Albany to Utica by train. The railroad ran right alongside the Erie Canal between the cities of Utica and Schenectady, and for the first time, the railroads were really competing with the canals. Alarmed by the prospect of rail travel taking business away from the canals, the New York State legislature passed a law that made it illegal for trains to carry freight. This ensured that all freight would be transported on the canals. As railroads became more common, however, attitudes changed. By the 1850s, the legislature allowed the Utica and Schenectady Railroad to carry freight.

Train travel was threatening the livelihood of the canals because the trains could follow routes that were beyond the reach of canals. Trains also offered a more luxurious ride than canal boats did, and they could transport goods and people more quickly than the boats could.

The Delaware and Hudson Canal opened in 1828, just three years after the completion of the Erie Canal. Benjamin Wright, the chief engineer on the Erie Canal, was also the chief engineer for this canal. The Delaware and Hudson Canal transported coal from Pennsylvania to the Hudson River.

The train tracks of the Erie Railway run beside the canal. This proximity of rail and water is not unusual; in

Mapmaker David Vaughan created this map in 1853 to illustrate the benefits of the enlarged canal, including its ability to handle bigger ships, which would enable it to compete with the railroads in the region.

fact, in many places, railroad tracks were laid right beside canals. This was because the land had already been cleared to build the canals, so it was faster and easier to build the train tracks there than to clear a new route.

The Erie Railway suffered financial problems from the time construction started in 1835. Many times it ran out of money and had to find new owners who could provide a financial boost. In spite of such problems, more and more tracks were laid, increasing the number of destinations that could be reached by train and, ultimately, taking business away from the canals.

LOOKING FOR A COMEBACK

Meanwhile, efforts to help the Erie Canal compete with the railroads continued to be made. In 1882, New York State abolished the tolls to reduce the cost of transporting freight on the canal. Discussion also arose about enlarging the canal again, so that it could handle larger boats carrying more freight. Though most people supported this idea, not everyone was happy about it. Widening the canal would require tearing down the many businesses that had sprung up along its banks. Some people were afraid that trains were going to get all the business anyway, so there was no point in spending money to enlarge the canal. Others were afraid that the expansion would reduce the value of farmland and other property along the canal. Still others worried that there would not be enough money to finish the project.

A public meeting to discuss the proposed expansion was held in New York City on December 29, 1885. Orlando

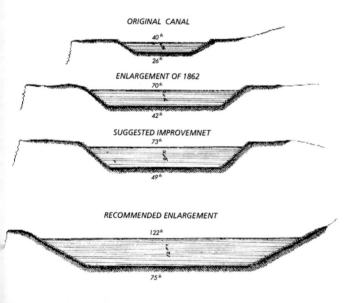

TYPICAL CROSS SECTIONS OF ERIE CANAL PRISM

ORIGINAL CANAL

40ᵗʰ

26ᵗʰ

ENLARGEMENT OF 1862

70ᵗʰ

42ᵗʰ

SUGGESTED IMPROVEMNET

73ᵗʰ

49ᵗʰ

RECOMMENDED ENLARGEMENT

122ᵗʰ

75ᵗʰ

From top to bottom, these drawings depict a cross-section of the original Erie Canal, another after its enlargement in 1862, and suggested improvements most likely used during discussions in the 1890s about another enlargement effort.

"IMPORTANCE OF IMPROVING AND MAINTAINING THE ERIE CANAL"

Almost immediately after Orlando Potter gave his speech, a four-page leaflet containing the speech was distributed around New York City and, possibly, throughout the state. Leaflets often dealt with current events, so it was important to get them printed and distributed while the public was still interested in a topic. The fact that this copy of the leaflet has O. B. Potter's signature in the upper left-hand corner of the first page suggests that Potter may have presented it to a friend.

Despite Potter's impassioned arguments, plans for the enlargement of the canal continued to face obstacles, and railroads increasingly took business away from canals. (For a transcription, see page 51.)

(For a transcription, see page 51.)

Compliments of

626

O. B. Potter

IMPORTANCE OF IMPROVING AND MAINTAINING THE ERIE CANAL BY THE STATE OF NEW YORK WITHOUT AID FROM THE GENERAL GOVERNMENT.

ADDRESS

OF

O. B. POTTER

AT A

PUBLIC MEETING HELD IN NEW YORK CITY,

DECEMBER 29, 1885.

FELLOW-CITIZENS :

I am glad to be present with you at this meeting. It is time we commenced the work resolved upon at the Utica conference, of lengthening the locks and deepening the Erie Canal, and putting it in a thorough state of efficiency. This canal has done more for the growth, development and prosperity of the State of New York, and especially of the city of New York, since its construction, than any other agency. If kept free, and in a state of efficiency, it will continue its work of beneficence and blessing to our State for generations. This canal is the only reliable security which the people of this State and of this great city and of our neighboring city of Brooklyn have that the vast commerce of the Mississippi Valley and of the Great Lakes shall continue to come in increasing measure to the port of New York, and through it to the outside world, at rates of freight which will enable New York State and this port and city to maintain their own place in the commerce of this continent and of the world. The line of the Erie Canal, with the Great Lakes, is the natural highway of commerce from the great valley of the Mississippi to the seaboard. It was given to this State by the munificent hand of the Creator for our development and use. If we are true to ourselves, it will continue to be the great highway of commerce from East to West upon this continent in the future as it has been in the past. I know it is said that the railways have superseded, and will supersede, the canal. I deny this proposition ; and maintain that however useful and important the railways (and no man holds their agency in advancing civilization in higher estimate than I do), they by no means supersede the necessity for the maintenance of our canal. The canal developed and called into being the great commerce by which our railways are now largely sup-

Brunson Potter was one of the speakers at the meeting. Potter was a wealthy and well-known New Yorker who owned a lot of property in New York City. From 1883 to 1885, he represented New York in the U.S. House of Representatives. Potter favored enlarging the Erie Canal, which he strongly believed was responsible for the state's prosperity. After saying how important he believed the canal was to the state's future, Potter responded to the two main objections to the project. He argued that the railroads had not taken the place of the canals and that they never would. In his vision of the future, the railroads and canals worked together to move goods and people around the country.

Potter also maintained that the canal enlargement would help farmers, not hurt them, since it would make it easier to ship agricultural products to towns and cities. At the end of his speech, Potter advised against asking the federal government to help pay for the project. He wanted the canal to remain New York's canal, a source of state pride and an example to the rest of the nation. He also warned that accepting money from the federal government would lead to higher taxes and to federal control over many state matters.

As the decision to enlarge the canal continued to be delayed, canals continued to lose business to railroads. In 1895, a decision was made. The state approved $9 million for the enlargement, despite protests that this would not be enough. Work on the project began soon after.

CHAPTER FIVE

THE ERIE CANAL IN THE MODERN AGE

The 1895 improvement project on the canal required locks to be lengthened, a deepening of the canal, and a modification of the aqueducts and most of the bridges. Many projected that it would require a good deal more than the $9 million allocated, saying that the enlargement could cost up to $15 million. As it turned out, the people who had worried that there would not be enough money to finish this second enlargement of the canal were correct. In 1898, short on funds and facing allegations of mismanagement, the project came to a halt.

THE BARGE CANAL ACT

For a while, no more progress was made on the canal enlargement, and some people thought that the canal would have to be abandoned. Then, around 1900, the federal government became interested in taking over existing canal systems for defense reasons as well as economic ones. The government wanted a channel connecting the Great Lakes and the Atlantic Ocean that could handle immense battleships and freighters. Such a channel would allow battleships to move quickly between inland waterways and the Atlantic Ocean in case of war. It would also benefit the national economy by allowing more freight to be transported more quickly. Congress had a study done to decide what to do. The final report recommended that Congress improve the Erie Canal. However, in spite of the report's recommendations, Congress never took any action.

Finally, New York's governor, Theodore Roosevelt, decided that the state should do something about the canal. In 1903, the New York State legislature passed the Barge Canal Act and approved borrowing money to build the Erie Barge Canal. This new canal would combine parts of the Erie Canal with new routes. The barge canal would also be much wider and deeper than the old canal, enabling it to handle much larger boats. In the end, the New York State Barge Canal System was 12 feet (3.66 m) deep, with new locks, whose gates were now motorized. Most lock sites also had a power plant.

Though the new canal carried a fair amount of canal traffic after it opened in 1918, things were not what they had once been. The peak year for traffic on the Erie Canal had been 1872. Every year after that, traffic on the canal decreased. Not only were there trains to compete with, but later on, highways

With no towpaths for horses along the Erie Barge Canal, packet boats could no longer be used. They were replaced by tugboats, such as the one seen here, which would tow larger barges and freighters.

were built and cars and trucks took over. The canal age had passed. Though the glory days of the Erie Canal were over by the end of the nineteenth century, the barge canal continued to carry freight for many more years.

THE ERIE CANAL IN SONG

"And you'll always know your neighbor,
You'll always know your pal,
If you've ever navigated on the Erie Canal"

So go some of the lyrics of the popular folk song "Low Bridge Everybody Down," also called "15 Miles on the Erie Canal," by Thomas S. Allen. Although the significance of the Erie Canal had dwindled by the early twentieth century, it lingered on in the popular imagination. This song describes the original Erie Canal and its importance in transporting goods out of New York to the Great Lakes.

Music also figured into the initial construction of the canal as well as its later enlargement efforts. Workers would make up songs to help pass the day. Those who later used the canal–boatmen, for example–would also dedicate songs or adapt songs of the sea. Theaters and music halls were built in some major cities along the canal. These drew crowds of passengers and canallers, spawning a lively entertainment circuit. The following are some other popular songs to emerge from the age of the Erie Canal and after:

- "The Meeting of the Waters/Ode for the Canal Celebration": This song was written specifically for the opening day of the canal on October 26, 1825. It was an adaptation of an earlier song, "The Vale of Avoca."

- **"Paddy on the Canal":** Irish immigrants, many of whom served as workers on the original canal and during its enlargement efforts, described their experience constructing the canal in this song.
- **"The Dark-Eyed Canaller":** This song was an adaptation of a sea shanty called "The Dark-Eyed Sailor." Boatmen who worked on the canal would learn such songs from sailors when they loaded or unloaded sea cargo.

Many other songs, poems, and stories immortalizing the canal survive to this day.

This hand-colored woodcut portrays bargemen working on the Erie Canal. Many of the songs such workers helped create and popularize are now considered American folk classics.

INTO THE TWENTY-FIRST CENTURY

After the end of World War II in 1945, the canal continued to be heavily used for about another six years. After that, the number of commercial boats using the canal began to decline. Finally, in 1994, commercial traffic on the canal came to an end.

As commercial traffic on the canal was diminishing, the state was working to promote other uses for the canal. In 1992, the state legislature created a special office called the New York State Canal Corporation to take care of the canal. In 1996, the Canal Corporation approved a $32 million plan to improve the canal for recreational uses. It planned to fix harbors and locks along the canal so that people with private boats could use them easily and safely. It also wanted to improve the almost 300 miles (483 km) of hiking and biking trails that line the canal. If many people used the canal for recreational purposes, then restaurants, hotels, and other businesses would open to serve them.

AN ENDURING SYMBOL

In an effort to preserve the rich heritage that had developed around the Erie Canal, the U.S. Congress established the Erie Canalway National Heritage Corridor in 2000. The corridor encompasses several canals in upstate New York, including the Erie, Cayuga-Seneca, Oswego, and Champlain canals. The historic canals, towpaths, and natural beauty of the 4,834-square-mile (12,520 square km) expanse are protected for residents and visitors alike.

In the course of eight years, the Erie Canal was transformed from "Clinton's Folly" into what many called the Eighth Wonder of the World. It became the

Each year the village of Waterford, New York, sponsors Canal Fest, which celebrates the Erie Canal. Although most of the vehicles now seen on the Erie Canal are recreational, the canal continues to draw many visitors.

focal point of nationalistic pride and exemplified the innovative and enterprising spirit that has long since been associated with the United States. Even in an age of fuel-efficient cars, air travel, and commuter rails, the Erie Canal stands the test of time.

TIMELINE

1808 Jesse Hawley proposes a canal to link Lake Erie and the Hudson River.

1817 DeWitt Clinton is elected governor of New York State. He persuades the legislature to authorize $7 million to build the Erie Canal first proposed by Hawley. Construction begins. Benjamin Wright is hired as chief engineer, James Geddes as assistant chief engineer, and Nathan S. Roberts as assistant engineer.

1819 The section of canal between Rome, New York, and Utica, New York, opens. Champlain Canal between the Hudson and St. Lawrence rivers opens.

1820 Planning begins on the "flight of five" at Lockport.

1825 The Erie Canal opens with celebrations across New York.

1826–1831 More canals open in New York, Pennsylvania, and New Jersey.

1835 Enlargement of the Erie Canal begins. Construction of the Erie Railway begins.

1836 Utica and Schenectady Railroad is completed. The state of New York forbids it to carry freight to prevent it from competing with the Erie Canal.

1862 The enlargement of the Erie Canal is completed.

1882 The state of New York abolishes tolls on the Erie Canal to help it compete with railroads.

1895 The second enlargement of the Erie Canal begins. It ends after three years because of lack of money.

1905 Work begins on much larger Erie Barge Canal, which will replace the old Erie Canal.

1918 The Erie Barge Canal is completed.

1994 Commercial traffic ceases on the Erie Barge Canal.

1996 The New York State Canal Corporation approves spending $32 million to improve the Erie Barge Canal for recreational use.

2000 U.S. Congress establishes the Erie Canalway National Heritage Corridor to preserve historic canals and related structures in upstate New York.

An Essay on the Enlargement of the Erie Canal

With Arguments in Favor of Retaining the Present Proposed Size of
Seventy Feet by Seven; and For Its Entire Length From Albany to Buffalo
Without Any Diminution

By Jesse Hawley
Lockport, N.Y.
Printed at the Courier Office.
1840.

Preface

The Enlargement of the Erie Canal was authorized under the Act of 11
May, 1835, by a Regency Legislature, possessing a majority of two to
one,—to be carried on by its surplus Tolls only.

In the party conflict for political capital, between a Whig Assembly
and a Regency Senate, the law of 18 April, 1838, was passed, authorizing
a loan of four millions, to accelerate the progress of the Enlargement.

Notwithstanding this liberal grant, a re-action—a sort of ebb-tide—
sat in against the measure, in which the politicians of both schools,
commenced an opposition to its further progress; and even residents
of the cities of New York and Albany, on whom the Canal had conferred
its greatest benefits, entered into public discussions, in the newspapers,
of both parties, and in both cities, opposing the measure as being of
dubious policy, and incurring an enormous state debt, and proposed to
reduce its dimensions, or limit its extent,—on which several motions
were made in the Legislature, then in session, in accordance with these
suggestions.

The session of 1839 closed without any definite Legislative action,
either to advance or, retard the progress of the work,—leaving those
hostile feelings to agitate and convulse the State with doubts, and
threats to arrest its future progress,—similar to the lowering aspect
which over-hung its original construction, from 1818 to the passage of
the two million bill, in Feb. 1821.

It was at this portentous hour the following Essay was written, — endeavoring to present a broad, perspicuous, and familiar view of the subject,—to spread it out, as on a Map, and to exhibit the Erie Canal, with its Enlargement, as the source of certain prosperity and future greatness to New York. It was drawn in the form of a Memorial, and presented to the House of Assembly, on 27 Jan., 1840, by Derick Sibley, Esq., from Monroe County, and referred to the Committee on Canals; and was, in part, included in the Report from that Committee, by G.W. Lay, Esq., from Genessee, on 28 March, 1840.

The very able and masterly Report of the Canal Board, of 9 April, 1840, soon came to the aid of Mr. Lay's Report. It was the former which mainly influence the Legislature to grant a further loan of two millions for the Enlargement of the Erie Canal, by the act of 24 April, 1840, and which goes so far to ensure its final completion.

With regard to the merits of the subject, I humbly acknowledge, that, with all my feeble labor and study, the theme is not half exhausted; — that the finite mind of man cannot comprehend the IMMENSITY of the future commercial and political benefits to flow from the construction of this navigable connexion—this New York Hellespont—between the American Mediterraneans and the Atlantic;—and I venture to predict, that the history of the anomalous opposition to the original construction and subsequent Enlargement of the Erie Canal, will be viewed by posterity as a Fable of antiquity.

J. HAWLEY
Lockport, 4 July, 1840
[...]

PAGE 27: TRANSCRIPTION OF KEY OF TABLE OF THE NEW RATES OF TOLL ON THE ERIE CANAL

Table of the New Rates of Toll on the Erie Canal, As established by the Canal board, and in effect on said Canal.
[Key at bottom of table]

4 Mills. On flour, salted beef and pork, bacon, butter, cheese, tallow, lard, beer and cider, pot and pearl ashes, window glass or glass ware, manufactured in this State, kelp, charcoal, broken castings, scrap iron and pig iron, stove, and all other iron castings, except machines and parts thereof, copperas and manganese, going towards tide water, sheep

skins, and raw hides of domestic animals of the United States, slate and tile for roofing, and stone ware, wool, rags and junk, manilla, wheat and all other agricultural productions of the United States not particularly specified, and not being merchandize, and all articles not enumerated or excepted, passing towards tide water.

3 Mills. On foreign gypsum, household furniture, carts, wagons, sleighs, ploughs and mechanics' tools, horses, (and each horse when not weighed to be computed at 900 lbs.) and corn.

2 Mills. On bran and ship stuffs, in bulk, stone, blocks of timber for paving streets, sawed lath, of less than ten feet in length, split lath, hoop poles, hand spikes, rowing oars, broom handles, spokes, hubs, tree-nails, felloes, boat knees, plane stocks, pickets for fences, and stuff manufactured or partly manufactured for chairs or bedsteads, and hop poles, brush handles, brush backs, looking glass backs, gun stocks, plough beams and plough handles, cotton, live cattle, sheep, hogs, horns, hoofs and bones, and pressed hay and pressed broom corn.

1 Mill. On gypsum, the product of this State, (not entitled to bounty,) brick, sand, lime, clay, earth, manure and iron ore, staves and heading, transported in boats, hemp and unmanufactured tobacco going towards tide water, and potatoes.

8 Mills. Merchandize not enumerated, and all other articles not enumerated or excepted, passing from tide water.

5 Mills. Sugar, molasses, coffee, nails, spikes, iron, steel, crockery.

3 Mills. On household furniture, accompanied by and actually belonging to families emigrating, carts, wagons, sleighs, ploughs and mechanics' tools necessary for the owner's individual use, when accompanied by the owner, emigrating for the purpose of settlement.

PAGE 39: TRANSCRIPTION OF AN EXCERPT FROM "IMPORTANCE OF IMPROVING AND MAINTAINING THE ERIE CANAL BY THE STATE OF NEW YORK WITHOUT AID FROM THE GENERAL GOVERNMENT," BY ORLANDO BRUNSON POTTER, SPEECH GIVEN DECEMBER 29, 1885

Compliments of O.B. Potter
Importance of Improving and Maintaining the Erie Canal By the State of New York Without Aid From the General Government.

Address of O. B. Potter at a Public Meeting Held in New York City, December 29, 1885.

FELLOW-CITIZENS:

I am glad to be present with you at this meeting. It is time we commenced the work resolved upon at the Utica conference, of lengthening the locks and deepening the Erie Canal, and putting it in a thorough state of efficiency. This canal has done more for the growth, development and prosperity of the State of New York, and especially of the city of New York, since its construction, than any other agency. If kept free, and in a state of efficiency, it will continue its work of beneficence and blessing to our State for generations. This canal is the only reliable security which the people of this State and of this great city and of our neighboring city of Brooklyn have that the vast commerce of the Mississippi Valley and of the Great Lakes shall continue to come in increasing measure to the port of New York, and through it to the outside world, at rates of freight which will enable New York State and this port and city to maintain their own place in the commerce of this continent and of the world. The line of the Erie Canal, with the Great Lakes, is the natural highway of commerce from the great valley of the Mississippi to the seaboard. It was given to this State by the munificent hand of the Creator for our development and use. If we are true to ourselves, it will continue to be the great highway of commerce from East to West upon this continent in the future as it has been in the past. I know it is said that the railways have superseded, and will supersede, the canal. I deny this proposition; and maintain that however useful and important the railways (and no man holds their agency in advancing civilization in higher estimate than I do), they by no means supersede the necessity for the maintenance of our canal. The canal developed and called into being the great commerce by which our railways are now largely supported; and there is no antagonism between these two great agencies. [...]

GLOSSARY

aqueduct A bridge used to carry flowing water across a river, road, or valley. Ancient Romans built the first aqueducts.

bushel A unit of measure of volume or capacity, used for dry agricultural products such as wheat. A bushel equals thirty-two quarts.

canal commissioner The government official responsible for regulating and maintaining canals.

canaller Someone who works on a canal.

civil engineer A person with the knowledge and skills needed to design and build structures such as canals, bridges, tunnels, and tall buildings.

crockery Dishes, pots, pans, and other similar items used in cooking or dining.

folly A mistake or unwise act.

freighter A ship that carries a large load of goods or cargo.

leaflet A printed and often folded piece of paper with information that is distributed for free.

legislature A body of elected officials with the power to make laws for a state or country.

lock An enclosure on a canal that has gates at both ends and is used to raise and lower boats as they move from one water level to another.

Louisiana Purchase The purchase of an enormous area of land between the Mississippi River and the Rocky Mountains by the United States from France in 1803.

nationalism A sense of loyalty and patriotism to a country.

packet boat A canal boat for passengers that also carried some mail and cargo.

surveyor A person who surveys, or measures, land.

toll A tax paid for using something like a bridge, road, or canal.

towpath The path beside a canal used by the animals pulling boats on the canal.

winch A machine that usually has a crank and can pull or lift heavy things with a chain or rope.

FOR MORE INFORMATION

The American Canal Society
Website: http://www.americancanals.org
The American Canal Society works to preserve and restore
the historic canals of the United States. Information and
publications are available through the organization's
website.

Canadian Canal Society
P.O. Box 23016
Carlton PO
145 Carlton Street
St. Catharines, ON L2R 7P6
Canada
Website: http://www.canadiancanalsociety.org
The Canadian Canal Society collaborates with other organi-
zations to document, restore, and preserve the historic
canals and waterways of Canada.

Canal New York
312 West Commercial Street
East Rochester, NY 14445
(585) 259-9283
Website: http://www.canalny.com
The goal of Canal New York is to bring business to the New
York State Canal System Corridor. The organization pro-
motes tourism and offers various educational outreach
and advocacy aid.

The Erie Canal Museum
318 Erie Boulevard East
Syracuse, NY 13202
(315) 471-0593

Website: http://eriecanalmuseum.org
Visitors will learn about the history and significance of the
Erie Canal at the Erie Canal Museum, which is located
in the only remaining weighlock building in the United
States.

The New-York Historical Society
170 Central Park West
at Richard Gilder Way (77th Street)
New York, NY 10024
(212) 873-3400
Website: http://www.nyhistory.org
The New-York Historical Society preserves the history and
culture of New York City and State and shares it with
the public through art exhibitions and public programs.
Its museum is the oldest in New York City.

Welland Canals Centre
1932 Welland Canals Parkway (at Lock 3)
St. Catharines, ON L2R 7K6
Canada
(905) 984-8880
Website: http://www.stcatharines.ca/en/experiencein/
WellandCanalsCentre.asp?_mid_=10025
The Welland Canals Centre at Lock 3 allows visitors to
observe Great Lakes ships on Lock 3. Visitors can watch
from an elevated platform or check out museum exhibits
and interactive displays describing the canal's history.

Western Erie Canal Alliance
44 Caroline Street
Clyde, NY 14433
(315) 923-9225

Website: http://www.westerneriecanal.com
The Western Erie Canal Alliance partners with local
    communities along the Western Erie Canal Heritage
    Corridor to preserve the historic and natural resources
    of the region and help develop local economies and
    culture.

WEBSITES

Because of the changing nature of Internet links, Rosen
Publishing has developed an online list of websites related
to the subject of this book. This site is updated regularly.
Please use this link to access the list:

http://www.rosenlinks.com/UAH/Erie

FOR FURTHER READING

Aller, Susan Bivin. *What Difference Could a Waterway Make?* Minneapolis, MN: Lerner Publications, 2011.

Drake, Patricia. *New York's Erie Canal*. New York, NY: Rosen Publishing, 2015.

Howe, Daniel Walker. *What Hath God Wrought: The Transformation of America, 1815–1848*. New York, NY: Oxford University Press, 2007.

Koeppel, Gerard. *Bond of Union: Building the Erie Canal and the American Empire*. Cambridge, MA: Da Capo Press, 2009.

McGreevy, Patrick. *Stairway to Empire: Lockport, the Erie Canal, and the Shaping of America*. Albany, NY: State University of New York Press, 2009.

McNeese, Tim. *The Erie Canal: Linking the Great Lakes*. New York, NY: Chelsea House, 2009.

Shank, W. H. *Towpaths to Tugboats: A History of American Canal Engineering*. York, PA: American Canal and Transportation Center, 1995.

Spanagel, David. *DeWitt Clinton and Amos Eaton: Geology and Power in Early New York*. Baltimore, MD: Johns Hopkins University Press, 2014.

Thompson, Linda. *Building the Erie Canal*. Vero Beach, FL: The Rourke Book Company, 2014.

Williams, Deborah. *The Erie Canal: Exploring New York's Great Canals*. New York, NY: W. W. Norton, 2009.

Winters, Donna, ed. *True Stories of the Erie Canal*. Garden, MI: Bigwater Publishing, 2012.

Wolmar, Christian. *The Great Railroad Revolution: The History of Trains in America*. New York, NY: PublicAffairs, 2012.

BIBLIOGRAPHY

Bernstein, Peter L. *Wedding of the Waters: The Erie Canal and the Making of a Great Nation*. New York, NY: W. W. Norton, 2005.

Doherty, Craig A., and Katherine M. Doherty. *The Erie Canal*. Woodbridge, CT: Blackbirch Press, Inc., 1997.

Encyclopædia Britannica Online. "Clinton, DeWitt." Retrieved November 13, 2014 (http://original.search. eb.com/eb/article-9024401).

Encyclopædia Britannica Online. "Erie Canal." Retrieved November 13, 2014 (http://original.search.eb.com/eb/ article-9032902).

Farley, Doug. "Erie Canal Discovery: The Jesse Hawley Story." *Lockport Journal*, December 1, 2007. Retrieved November 20, 2014 (http://www.lockportjournal.com/ opinion/erie-canal-discovery-the-jesse-hawley-story/ article_ab3d3d08-fe37-5049-8f91-0d31ba88c2f2. html?mode=story).

Find a Grave. "Jesse Hawley." Retrieved November 19, 2014 (http://www.findagrave.com/cgi-bin/ fg.cgi?page=gr&GRid=33904588).

Independence Hall Association. "The Canal Era." Retrieved November 15, 2014 (http://www.ushistory.org/us/25a.asp).

Larkin, F. Daniel, Julie C. Daniels, and Jean West, eds. *Erie Canal: New York's Gift to the Nation. A Document-Based Teacher Resource*. Albany, NY: New York State Archives Partnership Trust, 2001.

Marlin, Pam. "Jesse Hawley and the Erie Canal." My Hawley Family Blog. Retrieved November 25, 2014 (http://www .dmarlin.com/hawley/blog/march2012/index.html).

Murphy, Dan. *The Erie Canal: The Ditch That Opened a Nation*. Buffalo, NY: Western New York Wares Inc., 2001.

National Heritage Areas. "National Significance and Historical Context." Retrieved November 19, 2014 (http://www.nationalheritageareas.us/documents/

ErieCanalway07-2_National_Significance_Final.pdf).

Nelson, Pete. "Lost Book Dispatches: The Fate of
Charles Brodhead." *Adirondack Almanack*, March
30, 2013. Retrieved November 17, 2014 (http://
www.adirondackalmanack.com/2013/03/lost-brook-
dispatches-brodheads-fate.html).

Nelson, Pete. "Lost Book Dispatches: The Incredible Story
of Charles Brodhead, Surveyor." *Adirondack Almanack*,
March 16, 2013. Retrieved November 17, 2014 (http://
www.adirondackalmanack.com/2013/03/lost-brook-
dispatches-the-incredible-story-of-charles-brodhead-
surveyor.html).

New York City Department of Education Community School
District 28. "The Story in the Song: Teaching the Erie Canal
Through Music." *American Citizen: A School/Community
Consortium to Teach American History*, Winter 2009.
Retrieved November 25, 2014 (http://citylore
.dreamhosters.com/wp-content/uploads/2011/11/
gotham-newsletter_winter09.pdf).

New York State Canals. "Canal History." Retrieved
November 12, 2014 (http://www.canals.ny.gov/history/
history.html).

Root, Mary M. "The Building of the Erie Canal."
Backsights. Retrieved November 18, 2014 (http://www.
surveyhistory.org/building_the_erie_canal.htm).

Sadowski, Frank E., Jr. "The Erie Canal." Retrieved
November 13, 2014 (http://www.eriecanal.org/).

Whitford, Noble E. "History of the Canal System of the
State of New York, Volume I." Retrieved November 25,
2014 (http://www.eriecanal.org/texts/Whitford/1906/
Chap24.html).

INDEX

ABOUT THE AUTHORS

Lara Sahgal is a writer and editor based in New York City. She grew up near the Finger Lakes, where she learned about the New York State Canal System. She enjoys reading about local and regional history.

Janey Levy has a Ph.D. in art history from the University of Kansas. She has taught art history classes at several colleges and universities, published articles and essays on art history, and curated two art exhibits. She has written several books for Rosen Publishing.

PHOTO CREDITS

Designer: Michael Moy; Editor: Shalini Saxena